MW00592324

SPEND IT TWICE

A RETIREE'S GUIDE TO
FREE MONEY

MATT ZAGULA

WORD ASSOCIATION PUBLISHERS
www.wordassociation.com
1.800.827.7903

ISBN: 978-1-59571-459-6

Designed and published by

Word Association Publishers
205 Fifth Avenue
Tarentum, Pennsylvania 15084

www.wordassociation.com
1.800.827.7903

Forward

You hold in your hands a book that can change your life and insure your family's financial survival, even in the difficult times in which we live.

I know that's a tall order. I can just imagine you sitting there, thinking, "How can this book hold out such promise, even as the world around me seems to have gone mad?"

Let me give you a little background. My name is Bill Hammond and I am an elder law attorney. That means I help families who have a loved one facing a serious illness like Alzheimer's or Parkinson's, or families who have a loved one in a nursing home. As an elder law attorney, over the past decade I have helped thousands of families design plans to protect their loved ones and their finances. In some instances, this can mean dealing with very modest amounts of money and in others, dealing with families who are quite wealthy.

One of the characteristics my clients all share is that they want to protect their loved ones and make sure that they get the good care to which they are entitled. After that, they want to be sure that everything that they have worked for their entire life won't be lost to the cost of a catastrophic illness or a long-term nursing home stay.

Who can blame them? In fact, it was only when my mother-in-law suffered a stroke during a California earthquake in the mid 1990s that I began to understand the emotional and financial devastation that a long-term illness can cause.

My wife and I cared for her mother for a number of years, while raising five young children. I learned first hand the steps that families needed to take to protect their loved ones and their finances. Unfortunately, for my mother-in-law, I learned this too late.

Matt Zagula, author of *Spend It Twice*, has a different story. Matt and his wife are currently caregivers for Matt's mother-in-law, who suffers from Alzheimer's disease. Anyone who has cared for a loved one with Alzheimer's knows what a difficult burden this can be.

My story and Matt's story intersect here. I view these types of situations from a legal perspective. I see the heartbreak every day in my office in families who are trying to cope with a long-term care system that has run amuck. Matt sees these situations from a financial perspective. And while both sides of the coin are critical, Matt's financial expertise allows him to see solutions in ways that are outside the understanding of most attorneys. Matt has developed ways to allow families to protect their loved ones and their assets, regardless of the market environment.

When I got a call from Matt asking me to review *Spend It Twice*, my first reaction was that I would read it and that would be the end of that. Boy, was I wrong. This book has turned me into an evangelist. I want to tell every client that comes into my office about Matt's concept.

Matt has designed a plan to solve the biggest concern of middle-class Americans – the fear of losing their life savings to a long-term care crisis – and he has found the solution through an asset which almost all of us have – the family home. He shows you how to tap into this asset to safeguard your financial future, no matter what surprises the market may bring.

This is truly a visionary work. I have introduced it to my clients and I urge you to study it, highlighter in hand, so that you can also take action. Follow the advice in this book. Your children and your grandchildren will thank you for being wise enough and loving enough to take this step to protect yourself and to assure their financial future.

Read this book today and buy extra copies for those you love. It's that important.

As I mentioned earlier, the L.A. earthquake changed my life and shook things up in a way for my family that I could not have imagined before. I hope this book will be the force that shakes you out of your complacency and motivates you to take the steps you need to protect your loved ones and your finances. And the best part is that you can accomplish all of it by tapping into the hidden resources you already have that are just lying dormant.

Congratulations on finding *Spend It Twice*. Now, follow Matt's steps to protect yourself, your loved ones and your financial future.

William G. Hammond
Attorney at Law
Overland Park, Kansas

Dedication

Nothing good comes without effort and sacrifice. So, I want to dedicate this work to all of the people who made *Spend It Twice, A Retiree's Guide To Free Money* a reality.

First, to my wife and my son, Charlie, who sacrificed time with me so I could work on this book, which I believe is quite timely and critically important to retirees and those approaching retirement. I am hopeful that my time was well spent and that this book will help many American retirees better their financial position and the financial well being of their spouses and their families.

Professionally, this book never even gets a second thought by me without the friendship and professional relationship I have with Attorney Rick Law and Attorney Bill Hammond. *Spend It Twice* really started over breakfast with these two brilliant attorneys on a cold day in Denver, so thank you both for planting this seed.

Acknowledgements

The heavy lifting on the writing was done by Denise Beatty and Susan Mosley. Denise is a talented writer and without her efforts, none of this would have gotten done. Susan's contribution included a re-write that significantly improved the tone and read-ability of the text. I can't thank you both enough.

I appreciate that much of what I know is based on the experiences of my planning team, which includes my operations manager, Pam Weaver; funding coordinator, Alicia Licause; registered nurse, Anne Guio; eligibility specialist, Pat Cramblett, and attorneys Herman Lantz and Pam Smoljanovich.

In addition to my planning team I would also like recognize the members of The Longevity Planning Institute. These financial advisors have committed their time to learning the very best financial planning uses of *Spend It Twice* directly from the author.

To learn more about The Longevity Planning Institute go to: *www.lpibraintrust.org.*

Well, it's time. I hope you gain from *Spend It Twice* the necessary information you need to improve your financial situation. In life nothing is free, but you'll soon learn the outcome of the strategies contained in this book will create benefits where they didn't exist before. That's what I call Free Money. Enjoy!

SPEND IT TWICE

A RETIREE'S GUIDE TO
FREE MONEY

Chapter 1 How to Multiply Your Money with Free Money

Basically, the Free Money concept allows retired seniors to effectively create monthly income and/or create a larger distributable net worth. Let's break these options down for a moment. Many retirees could use some extra cash on a monthly basis. A steady flow of income is a necessity to comfortable retirement living. This needs no further explanation. Increasing net worth could use a little elaboration. This type of Free Money transaction increases net worth for the purpose of building a secure financial foundation for the retiree's spouse, children and grandchildren, who then get to spend the money again. In essence, they have a chance to *Spend It Twice*. The gift of financial freedom is one not many of us believe we can afford. But, you'll soon learn you can offer this gift without compromising your retirement income. It's truly *free* from infringing upon your retirement income and *free* from dipping into your retirement savings, so your current income and invested assets are not needed to create this additional income.

Before I explain further about how a retiree can *Spend It Twice* using Free Money, I want to give you more answers to the question, "Why seek free money at all?" The following information will provide substance, not fluff, so I encourage you to pay close attention. If you are a silver-haired senior or, perhaps, more recently retired, you may know some of the following details. But, you will be as surprised and concerned as I was when I first learned of these facts. This is where you and I travel down the statistical path of cold hard fact. I know there are some people out there who are financial factoid fanatics. For you, go ahead, jump in and read away. For those of you who are not, wrestle through this with me because these numbers contain a meaningful message that you need to know.

On average, Americans spent 19 hours planning for retirement last year. This is slightly more than the 11 hours spent planning for vacations and *equal* to the amount we Americans typically spend planning for our holidays.[1] Let's think about that one for a moment. Most of us will spend over 20 years in retirement. That's one-fourth of our life. If we're spending such an insignificant amount of time planning for our financial future – and some of us spend much less or no time at all – how thorough can our plan be? Many of us spent four *years* in college preparing for the future. Does it seem logical that we would then spend only 19 hours planning for retirement? Of course not, but those are the facts.

Many retirees don't feel the need to do much planning because they feel their loyalty to their employer will benefit them in their retirement years. But, here's a whammy - many employers are eliminating health care coverage for future retirees. Consider Ford Motor Company. If you worked for Ford over the past few generations, you believed you were set. Who wouldn't? You worked for a once hugely successful American industrial giant, the foundation and origin of the modern automobile and an innovator in automobile mechanics. It was a given as a Ford retiree, you could retire securely and enjoy your Golden Years. Enter foreign automakers, labor cost differences and employee benefit costs. The cost-strapped American giant had to find some way to survive against this new breed of fierce competitor, so they hit where it hurt the company the least, but affected their retirees the most – retiree benefits. Ford decided to remove retirees from their benefits plan in order

---

[1] *EBRI Issue Brief* No. 304, April 2007, www.ebri.org

to cut their costs and shift that cost burden to the individual retiree. As defined benefit pension plans become less available, personal savings and investments will become increasingly more important as the core for retirement funding. It will be critical for retirees to manage their assets prudently so they can produce sufficient income throughout their retirement. Sometimes, this is not so easy to do. Hopefully, in those 19 hours we allocate to planning our retirement, a few of us will figure out how to do that. For those who haven't, I encourage you to keep reading.

Let's take a look at the costs you'll face during retirement. Most of us envision spending our time visiting children and grandchildren who live a plane ride away, traveling to foreign shores to see what we didn't have time to see because we were busy working and raising a family or simply sinking that putt on our favorite 18th hole. To say the least, we want (heck, we deserve) to enjoy the fruits of a lifetime of labor. Ideally, we should be able to do some of these things. Some of us may have carefully thought out our monthly spending needs and calculated an allowance to enforce during these years (good for you!). However, in your best laid plans, I sincerely hope you considered health care costs. Health care costs are pretty consistent - they are always going up! And you must also consider that studies have found that 30% to 40% of us reaching age 65 will need nursing home care.[2] These facts alone should have you wanting to spend your money twice using a Free Money transaction. But if that's not enough, how about this? Assuming Medicare benefits remain at *current levels*, a married couple is expected to need approximately $300,000 to $550,000 to cover health expenses in retirement![3] Health care sure is a heavy financial burden.

In addition, longevity is a crucial factor in calculating your financial future. How many sunsets or sunrises do you

---

[2] "Lifetime use of nursing home care", *The New England Journal of Medicine*, Vol. 324 (February 18, 1991): 595-600

[3] "Savings Needed to Fund Health Insurance and Health Care Expenses in Retirement." *EBRI Issue Brief* No. 295 (Employee Benefit Research Institute, July 2006).

think you'll gaze upon? Studies show that a 65-year-old man today can expect to live to age 81, while a 65-year-old woman can expect to live to age 84.[4] Of course, there are those medical miracles who are still vibrant and active at 91. Point being, you can never be certain of your own longevity and how well you will feel at an advanced age. We may be living longer, but our quality of life may not be as we'd like. This is where that $300,000 to $550,000 number comes into play again and sparks in us the fear that we actually will outlive our money. And this fear is all so real today for many surviving spouses. Women face the most significant financial risk because, on average, they live longer.

Since we're talking long life, let's switch the discussion to what happens to our finances once we lose a beloved spouse. Statistics here suggest that many of you have painted a picture for yourself that is much *less* financially painful than your reality. It appears many think that their pocketbook won't be significantly affected when their spouse dies. A retirement survey found that only two in 10 retirees feel they would be financially worse off if their spouse were to die first. There appears to be a lack of awareness concerning the financial effects of becoming a widow. More than four out of 10 widows have no income other than social security.[5] When the income earning spouse dies, many times the widow loses the majority of the spouse's pension and takes a hit in their total household social security benefits. She loses her own social security income and receives her deceased husband's, if his is the higher value of the two, as is the case for the majority of married couples. Unfortunately, not only do we grieve for the loss of our loved ones, we later suffer financially from the loss of monthly income and the financial security that income provided.

---

[4] 2006 OASDI Trustees Report, Assumptions and Methods Underlying Actuarial Estimates, www.ssa.gov/OACT/TR/TR06/V_demographic.html#wp172303

[5] 2007 Risks and Process of Retirement Survey, 2007 Society of Actuaries' Key Findings: Risk of Retirement Report

Chapter 2 Dissecting the Anatomy of a Free Money Transaction & Unlocking the Secrets to Spending It Twice

The numbers in the first chapter can be quite sobering. And although those problems are the reality that many retirees face today, *you* have a resource here to help you maintain control of *your* financial future. Free Money is going to be placed right in front of you and although you may not know where or what it is yet, you soon will. More good news – Free Money is for almost *everyone*. Yes, almost everyone. Even if you are very well off financially, Free Money makes sense, just like it would make sense for the widowed retiree who just lost her husband's pension income and her own social security check. Also, no matter what your personal situation is, the general steps to complete a Free Money transaction are nearly the same and the results are significant. The decision to create monthly income with Free Money or to create distributable net worth for your heirs with Free Money is done at the end of a *Spend It Twice* transaction. Of course, you may choose a hybrid solution, such as the planning we will share with you in Chapter 3. There you will be introduced to Mim, who used her Free Money to buy a car, a cool new TV and a kitchen floor and then used the remaining Free Money to fund a special trust just for her grandchildren. Oops, I almost forgot. Mim also added an extra $10,000 to her savings account, just in case a rainy day came along.

But for now, let me explain how a retiree can truly spend their dollars twice by introducing you to the individual parts of a Free Money transaction. Free Money is the result of combining multiple financial transactions – it's not just one move. Therefore, the possibilities for you are nearly endless. But in order to understand how to discover your Free Money, three topics need some explanation: reverse mortgage, life insurance and annuities. All of the strategies discussed will use insurance-based products, so the outcome of your Free Money planning is not contingent on the stock market or CD rates. Let's examine the parts of this unique transaction individually and then move on to teach you how to not only claim your Free Money, but multiply your money for maximum benefit.

Reverse Mortgage: A Severely Underutilized Financial powerhouse Finally Revealed

Yes, I said powerhouse. Have some faith in me and keep reading. I understand your hesitation, because retirees, by and large, do not understand this mortgage product. Only 19% of retirees have used their homes to help fund their retirement. Now, out of that 19%, 53% actually sold their home to help out their retirement lifestyle. Only 5% of that 19% used a reverse mortgage. Mathematically, we are talking about less than 1% (specifically .95%) of retirees surveyed used a reverse mortgage to help fund their retirement. I believe that number is so low because what a reverse mortgage offers is not that good on a stand alone basis and falls short of what a healthy, vigorous senior needs and, more importantly, wants. But, that's where careful planning comes into play. The reverse mortgage is not the end result, but the funding source that gets the plan started. Before we get to the planning possibilities you really need to understand the basics of a reverse mortgage. Knowledge here is power, my friend.

Okay, reverse mortgage basics. You must be 62 years of age or older and have at least 50% equity in your home to qualify for a reverse mortgage. Free Money candidates must have at least 80% equity in their home, or, as is with the vast majority of retirees I work with, own their home outright. Unlike a standard mortgage where you have a payment, there is *no* payment due in a reverse mortgage at any point during your life while you are living in your home. To reinforce this key concept, you never have to pay back the mortgage while you are alive and living in your home. You also choose how the money comes out of your reverse mortgage – a monthly income, a line of credit, or a lump sum. Free Money plans *always* involve taking a lump sum. Most reverse mortgages are programs offered by the Federal Housing Authority (FHA) and the Department of Housing and Urban Development (HUD), programs funded by the US government.

Part of the cost of a reverse mortgage is the FHA insurance fee. When you and your spouse have passed away or sell the home, if the mortgage balance exceeds the value of the property, that insurance guarantees the lender that the government will pay off the excess debt. A reverse mortgage is a non-recourse debt meaning the lender has no recourse against you or your family. They must turn to the FHA to make up the difference between what you borrowed and the value of the house if, for instance, the value of the house has fallen below the balance of the mortgage. Reverse mortgages include insurance to make sure your family is not responsible for any part of the loan.

The reverse mortgage does *accrue* interest.

Accrued interest means that the interest just keeps rolling back into the loan. Remember, there is *no* payment, so the interest just gets added to the mortgage balance. This is a form of mortgage; it's not a new form of loan. Commercial real estate investors call this type of loan negative amortization. What is new is the amount of time that can pass without payment – your entire life or until you decide to leave or sell your home – that is unique. The house remains in your name. *You are not selling it*, you are borrowing against it. I know many retirees resist the idea of going into debt and that's one of the primary reasons reverse mortgages have failed to become popular. For you, though, this book will tell you all you need to know about how to use a reverse mortgage as a powerhouse financial planning tool.

A recent AARP/HUD study found that people use reverse mortgages for different reasons. The top three are:

1.) To pay health care costs.

2.) To pay off an existing mortgage.

3.) To reduce a financial burden on their children.

My Free Money concepts will open your eyes to these as well as many less-common uses. Plus, my reasons for using the reverse mortgage are a heck of a lot more fun than the top three listed above. Free Money is about living well, not about solving financial crises. So far, most people have used reverse mortgages to help them with severe financial problems. The reverse mortgage has not been properly used as the powerhouse *financial tool for planning purposes* that it truly is. *Spend It Twice* is about adding income and net worth to enhance your life, not about dealing with financial chaos. Claiming Free Money is about retirement enhancement, about optimism and family. It's planning bright with opportunity.

Reverse Mortgage Loan Facts

Benefits: 1.) You continue to live in your home and own your home.

2.) The money you receive from a reverse mortgage is *tax-free.*

3.) You can repay the loan at any time without penalty.

4.) You owe nothing as long as you live in your home.

5.) It's non-recourse – you have NO personal liability for repayment.

6.) The remaining equity in your home is for you to pass on to your intended beneficiaries

Costs: Although these are approximate figures for illustration purposes only and may vary, the costs are, typically, the following (based on the total transaction amount):

Fees (appraisal, termite, inspection, title)	1%
Origination Fees	2%
FHA Mortgage Insurance	2%
Realtor Commissions	0%
Total cost (Approx.)	5%

The most important thing a Free Money candidate needs to understand is that the reverse mortgage costs are pre-set and cannot be manipulated by the service providers. This is very important to understand. You can feel comfortable knowing that your costs are regulated by FHA guidelines and that the service provider you use cannot tamper with the pricing. The program was built by FHA to safeguard senior borrowers against potential lender fraud.

Reverse Mortgage Eligibility

1.) All borrowers must be 62 years of age or older and occupy the home as their primary residence.

2.) Any existing mortgages need to be paid off after the reverse mortgage is complete. Some retired homeowners with excessive debt may not be eligible.

3.) Town homes and condominium units can be eligible.

4.) Homes must meet HUD standards. If not, a reverse mortgage may still be possible with the repairs being a contingency of the loan post closing.

How Much Can Be Borrowed?

Well, the more your house is worth the more you can borrow, within certain limits. If your home is valued over $625,000, you may want to look into a jumbo reverse mortgage program (yes, that's actually what it's called). Again, this is just to familiarize you with the basics, so I won't elaborate.

Your loan amount will be based on a few key factors - the age of the youngest borrower, the appraised value of your home, the county in which your home is located, the current one-year US Treasury bill rate and your choice of program.

Because interest rates are based on the one-year US Treasury bill rate, rates are generally lower for a reverse mortgage than a traditional mortgage. Like I always say, a low interest rate is a good interest rate! Also, you can choose to have your rate adjusted monthly or annually. Interest rate changes after your closing *do not* affect your borrowed amount. Interest rate changes do affect the future balance of the loan – interest rates will either grow the balance faster during higher interest rate periods or slower based on a lower interest rate. A key concept to understand is that a Free Money transaction is not effected by future interest rate changes because your lump sum proceeds are "funded" to you tax free at your closing. To illustrate, let's assume at closing you receive $100,000. Future interest rate changes will not affect what you received because the loan is funded. However, the future balance will be dictated by interest rates as all interest in a reverse mortgage is accrued.

Who Repays the Loan?

At your death, your heirs can *choose* to sell the home and repay the loan. They can also keep any money from the sale of your home over and above the loan balance. If the reverse mortgage loan balance is $130,000 at your death and your home sells for $150,000 after expenses, then your kids keep the $20,000 of appreciation. It's important to know your family retains the value of your home's appreciation. *You are not selling your home to the government when you choose a reverse mortgage. It's a loan and you are still the owner.* Your estate has up to 12 months to repay the loan after you are gone, so your family has time to properly sell your home and avoid what is sometimes referred to as a "fire sale." This gives your family the time they need to get the best price for your home. But, you should know that your family is *not* responsible for the loan either because it is an asset based loan, meaning that if the loan balance far exceeds any possible sales price, they have the option to just walk away from the loan and your home with no financial consequence to them.

Matt, You Don't Understand.
I Want My Family To Get My House!

Actually, I do understand and it's one of the driving forces behind the *Spend It Twice* concept. This is one time where you will get your cake and be able to eat it, too. Your heirs can simply buy the house back at market value with the additional money you have left them. What money?? The Free Money! It exists and it is worth way more than the loan balance, but you'll only know how we do that financial wizardry if you keep reading.

Life Insurance,
Your Permission Slip To Financial Freedom

The only roadblock between you and a healthy stash of Free Money is your health. This brings us to our next step - life insurance - your permission slip to spend your money twice.

Remember how good it felt when you were in grade school and you had a hall pass. It was permission to move about the hallways of your school without risk. If a teacher stopped you, so what? You had the pass. It was freedom. You should consider life insurance your financial freedom pass when used with our Free Money concept. Sadly, today's retirees have been given the wrong impression about life insurance, much to their own financial detriment. Life insurance is retirement's *golden* hall pass. It is true freedom.

Let me present an example of this financial freedom by sharing my own estate plan with you. I have a trust which contains a healthy amount of life insurance, more than enough to take care of my wife and son for life. The trust is *not* identified by my social security number, but has its own identification number. The trust is set up this way because it creates potential tax benefits. When I die, Uncle Sam may want a cut of my estate, but the government can't have any of my trust money because it's outside of my estate. For those of you who live in states that have a death tax, you should check with an attorney to see if there are ways to avoid it. By the way, do-it-yourself estate planning is a really bad idea. Don't ever let anyone tell you that you don't need an attorney. You do, so find a good one. Sure, you're going to get a bill, but those folks are worth the money they charge. A good estate and elder planning attorney can really make the difference in your overall estate and long-term care planning.

Back to my plan. I have a unique life insurance policy directly insuring me and then a larger, more traditional policy owned by my trust. The unique insurance pays when I die or it pays a benefit if I become disabled and need care. But, my trust is set up a little differently. My wife gets the income, but *not* the principal from that death benefit. The reason, simply, is that if she goes into a nursing home, the money in my trust could well be gone, spent down on her long-term care expenses and, thereby, essentially making a nursing home and not my son the primary beneficiary of my life insurance. Another reason I don't own the larger life insurance policy directly is because if I go into a nursing home, the state will consider the cash value from my policy as a resource available for payment to the nursing home and force my family to take the cash value out of the insurance policy to pay for my long-term care expenses. Then, the life insurance death benefit will collapse and my plan will fail. This is why I have the unique coverage I do. It provides up to $10,000 per month for my long-term care needs and could last as long as 50 months, if necessary. Stay with me, because I'll go into great detail in a later chapter about exactly how to do this. I have planned this way because it's important to me not to accept a small retirement. I want to live my later years to the fullest and *still* leave plenty of money for my family so they, too, will live very, very well. I don't want them to want for anything, so I built a plan that is beneficial for all of us. Another way to explain my planning is that I want to live rich, die broke, and very soon afterwards have a large life insurance check delivered to my home, making my wife and son financially well off again. The plan is extremely well thought out and life insurance is at the heart of it. I get to spend my retirement money and then have it all come back when I die so that my family can spend it again. So, my retirement money gets spent twice.

You see, my trust-owned life insurance policy is MY permission slip, MY hall pass to move around and do what I want because *I truly do plan on spending all of my money over my lifetime.* I won't have any risk of outliving my money and I'll create wealth that will last for my family because of my progressive life insurance and trust planning. I'll explain in just a few pages how my income will be guaranteed, when I introduce you to the immediate annuity. But first let's get some clarity.

Life Insurance is Confusing. I Don't Understand It?

I have heard this said a time or two. People wonder, "Should I buy term life insurance, whole life insurance, universal life insurance or variable life insurance?" How does life insurance work? Well, let me simplify it for you. If you bought this book, forget term life insurance, whole life insurance and variable life insurance. They just don't work in the Free Money strategies. Only universal life insurance works. Term life is only applicable for a stated period of time. The key to the Free Money concept is to be sure the coverage is in place when you die so your heirs have access to the money at the time when it is needed the most. Whole life insurance is a great concept, but it costs a fortune because it's designed to cover your 'whole lifetime' and the required premium outlay is prohibitive. Universal life insurance is guaranteed to a selected age chosen by you. Therefore, the premiums can be adjusted for a shorter time span. Variable life insurance is based on stock market rate of return variables and usually is not acceptable for Free Money use. The cash value in a universal life policy is largely irrelevant to this type of planning because we are buying life insurance coverage for a period of time, which can be guaranteed forever based on the purchase of available riders. Purchasing universal life insurance provides a stable stated death benefit that is determined at the time of issue. It is a perfectly structured life insurance policy for a *Spend It Twice* plan.

To be fair, you, the reader, may be confused in this area and the insurance companies don't always help bridge the knowledge gap. The general consumer needs to employ a very savvy insurance advisor. Assuming you don't have access to such an expert in this field, let me share a few life insurance buying tips that can make you a more informed buyer. Insurance companies offer fully guaranteed products that are terrific for a Free Money transaction. With universal life insurance, you can pick a guaranteed coverage period. So, the premium to guarantee life insurance coverage to age 100 and beyond can be 15% to 30% more expensive than to, say, age 85 or 90. From an actuarial standpoint, not many people live to be 100 or older, so paying for a guarantee of coverage to age 100 may not be financially sensible. Significant savings could be had by paying for coverage to a more realistic age – like, for instance, 85 or 90.

But, having an absolute guarantee is very important to most because accepting the longevity risk can become too stressful to accept and, therefore, it is best for the individual to shift the risk onto the insurance carrier and buy the absolute lifetime guarantee. So, my mathematical mind won't let me say the lifetime guarantee is the absolute right way to do this. It's a matter of either accepting the longevity risk or transferring it. I'm conservative, so I prefer the lifetime guarantee. However, an emerging trend is to hire a personal actuary to assess your medical records and family history to make a more educated guess about how long you may live and, thereby, giving you a better gauge of the time span your universal like insurance policy will cover. Again, this is always a decision made by the Free Money benefactor. *But when in doubt, it's best to have a guarantee and with the leverage the Free Money allows us, a guarantee is a luxury we can afford.*

How Much Life Insurance Can I Buy and How Much Will It Cost?

Remember, Free Money is about you, so let's not use the word cost. We are using the life insurance to replace or enhance the value of your home in the Free Money transaction. As I mentioned earlier, in Chapter 3 I'll introduce you to Mim's transaction, which explains the Free Money concept in its purest and most perfect form. Mim was able to get a few basic items she needed through her Free Money transaction plus an additional stash of $10,000 deposited into her savings and a trust benefiting her grandchildren funded with $215,600 of life insurance. You'll see that she was able to get the items she really wanted and still increase the value of her house for the benefit of her family by creating 66% more distributable net worth than the value of the home. Also, she has a newly created 50-month long-term care benefit worth $4,312 per month that she can use for home health, assisted living or skilled nursing care, if needed.

Single Payment Universal Life

Universal Life becomes more enticing when purchased with a single payment. Let me break down a few examples to show you how much sweeter trust planning funded with a single payment becomes for your heirs.

$100,000 Lump Sum Contribution				
	Male – Preferred NT		Female – Preferred NT	
Age Purchased:	Death Benefit Without Life Access Accelerated Benefits Rider	Death Benefit With Life Access Accelerated Benefits Rider	Death Benefit Without Life Access Accelerated Benefits Rider	Death Benefit With Life Access Accelerated Benefits Rider
Age 65	$ 340,653	$ 315,376	$ 403,567	$ 351,762
Age 75	$ 222,256	$ 205,986	$ 268,447	$ 238,691
Age 80	$164,757	$ 153,949	$ 187,848	$ 170,359
Age 85	$126,138	N/A	$ 134,366	N/A

In a Free Money transaction, you can substantially increase your distributable net worth by leveraging the use of the proper life insurance product in your plan. The results can be truly amazing, if you qualify for the coverage.

Immediate Annuities,
Creating Income That You Can't Outlive

The first chapter presented statistics on how retirees may actually outlive their assets. It's a substantial risk and the thought is very frightening. As we age, our expenses can increase. Health care costs alone can be staggering. Remember the $300,000 to $550,000 worth of healthcare expenses during retirement alone? However, the most bothersome misconception revealed is that a surviving spouse will be able to lead a lifestyle comparable to the one they had while their spouse was alive. This is far from reality. So, making income last a lifetime is a critical part of retirement planning.

The Social Security Shuffle

Ahhh, government's solution for the aging American. The idea behind social security was fabulous, providing money on a monthly basis to help our senior community during its Golden Years. But, the reality is that with costs on the rise, social security only goes so far and stand alone social security is not enough to survive on these days!

Even living off a dual social security income in a married situation isn't easy without supplemental income, like a company pension, interest from savings or dividends from investments. Things can, and often do, get much worse. When you lose your beloved spouse, the government rules place you into what I call the 'Social Security Shuffle'. Now, this isn't a fancy new dance step, but the beginning of the shuffling of your income. That's right, Uncle Sam sends you a letter explaining they will now discontinue sending the lower of the two social security checks.

Let's look at a simple example.

Beth and Roger are a married couple. Roger gets $1,300 of social security income and Beth gets $525. If Roger dies before Beth, what happens? Well, Beth "inherits" Roger's social security check of $1,300. However, she does *not* get to retain her own social security check of $525. She gets the larger of the two and, therefore, the household income drops at Roger's death by her social security amount of $525 per month.

Now, that usually is not the extent of the financial loss caused by the death of a spouse. Let's also assume that Roger had a pension from his industrial job. His defined benefit pension was $1,100 per month. Typically, one of three scenarios take place in the status of the deceased's pension:

1.) The pension is a straight life pension and Beth will get nothing. The pension dies when the participant dies.

2.) The surviving spouse is named as a percentage beneficiary and the monthly benefit is a percentage of the original pension. For example, if Roger chose a 50% pension for his wife, his own pension was probably reduced from $1,100 to, perhaps, $980. So, a 50% survivor pension benefit for Beth would mean her new pension income would be 50% of Roger's $980 or $490 per month.

3.) Survivor is when the surviving spouse would get 100% of the deceased's pension. In Beth's case, that would mean she would get 100% of Roger's monthly pension. Now, by choosing with this option, Roger's pension would have been significantly reduced from the straight pension amount of $1,100 to, maybe, $780 per month. These figures are only guesstimates because each defined benefit plan is built differently and the plan's actuarial assumptions define these figures. The numbers given here are just to give you an idea of how different pension setups work.

Let's look at the household income if Roger dies and Beth had a 50% survivor pension:

Roger living - $980 pension
                 + $1,300 social security
                 + $525 Beth's social security
                 = $2,805 of household income
Roger deceased - $1,300 "inherited" social security
                 + $490 50% pension
                 = $1,790 of household income

Beth's overall household income is reduced by *over 36%!* That is a significant loss. So much for gasoline and Christmas presents for the grandkids!

It's also necessary to consider the impact of what health insurance will cost Beth, especially if Roger's retirement plan does not provide a widow's health care coverage plan. The cost can be financially devastating. But, what if Roger and Beth recognized this problem and wanted to solve it without compromising their retirement? What if they were comfortable with their retirement income, but wanted to prevent this potentially serious financial shortfall? What could they do? Let's assume they own a $100,000 market value home in West Virginia, are both age 73 and purchased a copy of this book to apply the Free Money concept to their situation. Their first step would be to apply for a reverse mortgage. Below you will see the results of the current Wells Fargo on-line reverse mortgage calculator:

Your information
Borrower(s) Date of Birth: 2/1/1935; 5/15/1935
Home Value and Location: $100,000; 26062 BROOKE
Total Property Loans and Liens: $0

Results

	HECM Monthly	HECM Annual
Lump Sum Advance		
Total Funds Available	$70,100	$58,700
Net Funds Available	$59,491	$48,632
Or a Credit Line Account		
Credit Line Available	$59,491	$48,632
Annual Growth Rate	3.5%	4.85%
Potential credit line in five years	$70,850	$61,948
Potential credit line in ten years	$84,378	$78,910
Or a monthly advance for as long as you live in your home		
Monthly Funds Available	$385	$356
Or any combination of lump sum at closing, credit line account, and monthly advance		

As you can see, the HECM monthly loan produces the largest lump sum offer. HECM stands for Home Equity Conversion Mortgage and is an FHA product. The monthly adjusted rate always produces the largest loan available because it allows the lender greater flexibility to adjust your interest rate as the rates fluctuate. This does *not* necessarily mean you will accrue more interest. You may pay more *or* you may also pay less. Your loan simply adjusts more frequently, protecting the lender from quick interest rate changes. Although for Free Money purposes, this is not a significant factor since we want to maximize the lump sum at the time of the transaction. If a fixed interest rate is available, it may give you a larger lump sum payment, but usually eliminates other payout options.

Through the reverse mortgage process, Roger and Beth can receive $59,491 in a lump sum from their $100,000 house. We already know Beth is at risk from an income standpoint, so the practical move in their situation is to use the Free Money to buy life insurance on Roger using the whole $59,491.

Because they are comfortable with their retirement income, that $59,491 could buy Roger $155,096 worth of life insurance benefits, payable on his death. If he is in preferred physical condition, that amount of coverage could be as high as $206,182. Now after Roger is gone, Beth will have a lump sum of $155,096 (we'll use this amount assuming his health is typical and not preferred). We'll also assume Roger and Beth have no children. Because there are no future heirs, the insurance policy should be held in trust for the sole benefit of Beth and the terms of that trust could dictate that at her husband's death, she would be able to buy an income producing annuity. The type of annuity Beth should buy is called an immediate annuity. You can buy immediate annuities in many different forms. The most common forms of immediate annuities are:

1.) **A Life Only Immediate Annuity** - this type of annuity is for the life of the annuity owner. The income paid from the annuity expires at the death of the annuitant. With this type of contract the annuitant assumes a portion of the longevity risk, but also has significant gain if his or her lifespan far exceeds the norm. To illustrate, we'll assume our annuity buyer is an 82-year-old male. The 1980 Commissioners Standard Life Expectancy Tables establish his normal mortality to be 6.18 more years. If this 82-year-old male lives to be 100, 12 years beyond the standard life expectancy, chances are very good that no other investment could even come close to the guaranteed yield the life only immediate annuity provided him. Conversely, if he died within three years from the date of purchasing the annuity, he would have received monthly income in return. But, the monthly income paid out would be less than the amount funded into the annuity. Obviously, this is not the desired outcome we are looking for. The longevity risk of a life annuity is certainly a gamble. You may win big, but you may also lose. It just depends on how long you live.

2.) **Period Certain Annuity** - this type of annuity pays out for a specified period of time. If, for instance, you buy an annuity that will cover a five-year term, it will pay out in equal installments for 60 months. The payout is not affected by the stock market, interest rates or CD rates and is guaranteed by the insurer to stay the same for the life of the contract. If you own a five-year period certain annuity with a monthly benefit of $1,200, you will get $1,200 per month for 60 months.

3.) **Life with Installment Refund Immediate Annuity (also called Life with Period Certain)** - This is a hybrid of the two annuity types described above. With this type of annuity the payments are guaranteed for life, just like the life annuity. The twist is, if you die prior to all of your money being paid back, the insurer guarantees that the annuity will continue to pay out until you or your beneficiary (after your death) receive at least the initial invested amount.

Given this information, the annuity that provides Beth with the greatest potential yield throughout her retirement would be the life only annuity. Keep in mind, Beth may still consider the life with installment refund annuity if she wants to preserve money for a niece, nephew, friend, favorite charity or any other beneficiary. That notwithstanding, the life annuity is the best payout option.

If we assume Roger dies at age 83 with his death benefit of $155,069 in place and the proceeds are then used to purchase a life annuity, Beth would receive $1,884.97 of monthly income. Imagine if Beth, now age 83, lives to be 100. She would receive a total of $384,533 in annuity benefit payments! It's important to note that the taxable portion of Beth's income is only $196.04 per month. This means out of Beth's $22,619.64 of annual income, she will receive a 1099 tax form requiring her to report only $2,352.48 of taxable interest earned until she receives back *all* of her original contribution ($155,069). Only after the full $155,069 is paid to Beth would the full $1,884.97 of monthly income be taxable. This taxation change occurs when your entire initial basis has been paid out to you in the form of income, meaning when all of the money that you deposited into the annuity is returned to you. What you get after that has to be interest income because your entire principal has been returned. Of course, Beth has options to design her trust to allow added flexibility. She could choose how much she wants distributed from her trust as retirement income and how much of the money she wants to put into her liquid savings account. Free Money creates an abundance of wealth of flexibility and options. Oh, and most importantly, it creates wealth and with money to work with, we have options! Like my good friend Atty. Rick Law says, "You know, when you're out of money, you're out of options and I never want to have a client out of money and out of options." Amen, Rick. Free Money is about having money in the right place at the right time.

That does it for the parts of the transaction. Hopefully, you've learned a lot of the information you'll need to help you see your Free Money opportunity unfold in the stories that follow. Now you can test your new found knowledge on the upcoming case studies. This will allow you to see Free Money in action. Studying the transactions of others will help you better see if Free Money is right for you. From this point forward, we will focus on case studies where the financial outcome is tailored to the needs and desires of the folks that we served. There are unlimited outcomes that can be achieved when employing Free Money. Your outcome, ultimately, would be tailored to your specific situation at the time of planning. My goal throughout the next few chapters is to help you see the opportunity and more thoroughly understand how Free Money can enhance your life.

Chapter 3 Mim's Free Money

Important Disclosure: Please be advised that all of the case studies in the following chapters are real life applications of how a Free Money transaction can work. However, the author has scrambled the facts and names to protect the privacy of our clients Confidentiality is one of our firm's highest priorities.

Mim's planning was quite complete. Her husband was a brilliant man devoted to his wife and family. They had a relationship that ladies read about in romance novels. When Mim became a widow, she fully understood that her spouse's love for her was multi-faceted and included his strong desire to protect her well beyond his lifetime. His plan included a 15-year period certain annuity to supplement her income of his social security and company pension. Her total income was more than sufficient by most retiree standards, but...

Mim is a wonderful mother and grandmother. We often pleaded with Mim to pull back on her spending - almost all of which was for her family. However, spoiling her beautiful grandchildren and helping her kids is what makes Mim the happiest. Mim's children are all accomplished professionals and well off financially. But Mim, like most moms, insisted on giving to them anyway. She bought extravagant Christmas gifts for her babies and insisted on slipping them "just a little" money on a regular basis. So, even though Mim makes her financial ends meet with her retirement income, there came a time when she needed a few things for herself - like a new car, a new TV and a kitchen floor to replace the one that served her throughout all those years of raising her children. Mim was facing some financial requirements that she needed to address. Her income was adequate, but really didn't give her the financial wiggle room she needed to make these home repairs and continue being so generous to her family.

Enter Free Money! Mim's house in Ohio was appraised for $130,000. Based on the Reverse Mortgage Calculator results from Wells Fargo - *www.wellsrm.com* - we received the following data:

Your information

Borrower(s) Date of Birth: 4/2/1937

Home Value and Location: $130,000; 43952 JEFFERSON

Total Property Loans and Liens: $0

Results

	HECM Monthly	HECM Annual
Lump Sum Advance		
Total Funds Available	$91,780	$72,930
Net Funds Available	$79,537	$61,394
Or a Credit Line Account		
Credit Line Available	$79,537	$61,394
Annual Growth Rate	4.23%	5.83%
Potential credit line in five years	$98,233	$82,113
Potential credit line in ten years	$121,325	$109,826
Or a monthly advance for as long as you live in your home		
Monthly Funds Available	$486	$439
Or any combination of lump sum at closing, credit line account, and monthly advance		

We found the HECM monthly loan produced the best lump sum advance available at $79,537. Now, we had to figure out how we were going to allocate those dollars into a Free Money transaction to allow Mim to meet her needs and, just as important, still do the things she wants to do, thereby allowing Mim to *Spend It Twice*.

As we said, Mim needed a new car. Her Pontiac was failing her and was constantly in the repair shop. Her children were concerned about her safety and wanted her to buy a used Toyota so that she would have reliable transportation. Initially, Mim didn't like the idea, but as the repair bills accrued and the car spent more time at the dealership's garage than her own, she finally came around to the idea. A new car with her trade-in would require about $17,000. While Mim and her boys shopped around, her daughter coordinated a meeting with a local flooring company to quote the job of replacing the kitchen floor - $3,000. At the same time, Mim found a TV she really loved at Best Buy for $2,000 – an HDTV! In all, Mim was going to use twenty-two thousand of her Free Money dollars to *enhance her life*. With $22,000 accounted for and $79,537 available, some additional opportunities presented themselves.

A few years back, Mim created an irrevocable trust for the benefit of her children. The trust owned a life insurance policy on Mim for a significant $1,000,000 death benefit payable to her children. The amount was determined by her husband's "dream" of taking care of Mim, first, and still one day leaving $1,000,000 for his children. His first goal was to be sure Mim would be well taken care of, but he still believed it was possible to leave a large estate behind to benefit the kids as well. The life insurance held within her asset protection trust guaranteed that would happen. Mim loved this aspect of her planning. However, as we continued to talk about her Free Money transaction, she became intrigued with the idea of setting up a smaller trust just for her grandchildren. At 71, Mim could use $50,000 of Free Money to buy life insurance coverage guaranteed through age 90 and funnel it into a trust for her grandchildren. This created a final "gift" worth over $248,000 upon her death. Because this "gift" is funded by a life insurance benefit, the final benefits paid out to the grandchildren would be totally tax free and the trust insured it would not have to go through probate. Also, because Mim was trust savvy, she knew the trust would be protected from any long-term care crisis 60 months after the life insurance was transferred into the trust. I want you to imagine Mim's face when we shared these numbers with her. After a big "wow" she asked, "So, you are telling me that we use $50,000 of that Free Money and my little ones get $248,648?" I simply responded "yep" and she let out another "wow." Nothing is better than helping good, hard-working people claim Free Money. I then had to tell her, with much pleasure, that she would have some money left over - $7,537 - that she might want to put that into her savings account - just in case she needed a little extra cash.

Mim was blown away because:

1.) She got what *she needed and wanted* – a new car, TV and kitchen floor plus a huge financial "gift" for her grandchildren.

2.) She got *more value from her home* - her home equity funded a trust worth *$118,848 more* than her house appraised for → $248,648 minus the house value of $130,000. She was able to spend the dead equity in her house and then give it to her grandchildren. That's "*Spending It Twice!*"

3.) She realized that her children get any value over and above the mortgage when the house sells after her death → *more Upside Potential for Her Family.*

4.) She relished the fact that her children *were not responsible* for the mortgage balance. She already knew that *none of her kids wanted the house because they already had homes of their own.*

Don't you just love happy endings? This is just one example of how Free Money can literally extract the hidden wealth contained within your own walls. Keep going. There are more examples to follow with even more exciting retirement-enhancing benefits to learn about.

Chapter 4 Learn How a $250,000 IRA Can Turn into $1.4 Million Tax Free!

Of all the *Spend It Twice* strategies, I love this one the most! It's not nice to pick favorites, but the wealth this transaction creates can be astronomical. This concept is so straightforward and powerful that when I shared it with a group of leading elder law attorneys, they were *almost* speechless. But, one great comment did emerge and it was, "say goodbye to Required Minimum Distributions."

Now, some of you might not know about Required Minimum Distributions (RMD). RMDs happens when you have an IRA and turn 70½ years of age. The government literally requires you to take out money and pay income tax on your distribution. The IRA is an awesome accumulator because it grows tax deferred. But, Uncle Sam says enough is enough at age 70½. At that age, you need to take out at least the required distribution based on your age. Of course, you can always take more.

IRS Uniform Lifetime Table (ages 70 – 115+)

Age of IRA Owner	Distribution Period (Years)	Age of IRA Owner	Distribution Period (Years)	Age of IRA Owner	Distribution Period (Years)
70	27.4	85	14.8	100	6.3
71	26.5	86	14.1	101	5.9
72	25.6	87	13.4	102	5.5
73	24.7	88	12.7	103	5.2
74	23.8	89	12.0	104	4.9
75	22.9	90	11.4	105	4.5
76	22.0	91	10.8	106	4.2
77	21.2	92	10.2	107	3.9
78	20.3	93	9.6	108	3.7
79	19.5	94	9.1	109	3.4
80	18.7	95	8.6	110	3.1
81	17.9	96	8.1	111	2.9
82	17.1	97	7.6	112	2.6
83	16.3	98	7.1	113	2.4
84	15.5	99	6.7	114	2.1
				115+	1.9

For your convenience, I converted these life expectancy tables to percentages as an easier way to understand them.

IRS Uniform Lifetime Table (Converted to percentages)

Age of IRA Owner	Required Minimum Distribution	Age of IRA Owner	Required Minimum Distribution	Age of IRA Owner	Required Minimum Distribution
70	3.6496	85	6.7567	100	15.8730
71	3.7736	86	7.0921	101	16.9492
72	3.9062	87	7.4626	102	18.1818
73	4.0485	88	7.8740	103	19.2308
74	4.2016	89	8.3333	104	20.4082
75	4.3668	90	8.7719	105	22.2222
76	4.5455	91	9.2592	106	23.8095
77	4.7169	92	9.8039	107	25.6410
78	4.9261	93	10.4166	108	27.0270
79	5.1282	94	10.9890	109	29.4118
80	5.3475	95	11.6279	110	32.2581
81	5.5865	96	12.3457	111	34.4483
82	5.8479	97	13.1579	112	38.4615
83	6.1349	98	14.1845	113	41.6667
84	6.4516	99	14.9254	114	47.6190
				115+	52.6316

Let me give you a quick explanation. As you can see, the Uniform Tables say that an IRA owner age 70 who is married has a joint life expectancy of 27.4 years. If the IRA value was $100,000, you would divide the $100,000 by 27.4 years and the RMD would be $3,649.63. The above table allows you to multiply the value of your IRA on the preceding December 31st by the proper percentage thus arriving at the correct RMD. Hopefully, the tables now make good sense to you.

Generally, people know that after age 70½, IRA owners *must* take distributions. The vast majority of retirees subjected to the RMD does not agree with this requirement and would be thrilled if they could just keep accumulating the IRA value on a tax deferred basis. But, IRAs don't offer their owners that option and missing an RMD carries a 50% tax penalty. That's not a misprint – 50% of the missed amount of the RMD. If you were required to take out $4,000 and you neglected to do so, then you owe the IRS $2,000 as a penalty payment for missing that distribution and that doesn't even take into consideration that you still owe income tax on the full $4,000. So, ignoring your RMD isn't an option – the penalties are very stiff.

We need to ask, does an option exist to free IRA owners from RMDs? Is it possible to take taxable money and convert it into tax free wealth? The Free Money answer is truly amazing.

Imagine a couple named Edward and Bonnie. Edward is age 73, Bonnie is 71. Ed and Bonnie have one son named David, age 48. From an asset perspective we will focus only on Ed's IRA of $250,000 and Ed and Bonnie's home, which is valued at $225,000 and has no outstanding mortgage. To illustrate this wealth creation concept, income is not relevant and we can ignore "other" assets. Let's just look at the Free Money effect when we convert an IRA to a Roth IRA.

The following table assumes Ed's age of 73, Bonnie's age of 71, David's age of 48 and a 6% constant rate of return.

**IRS Uniform Lifetime
Minimum Distribution Table**

Year	Pension Fund Begin Value	Life Expectancy	Minimum Distributions
2008	$250,000	24.7	$10,121
2009	$254,272	23.8	$10,684
2010	$258,203	22.9	$11,275
2011	$261,744	22.0	$11,897
2012	$264,838	21.2	$12,492
2013	$267,487	20.3	$13,177

2014	$269,569	19.5	$13,824
2015	$271,090	18.7	$14,497
2016	$271,989	17.9	$15,195
2017	$272,202	17.1	$15,918
2018	$271,661	16.3	$16,666
2019	$270,295	15.5	$17,438
2020	$268,028	14.8	$18,110
2021	$264,913	14.1	$18,788
2022	$260,893	14.8	$17,628
2023	$257,861	14.1	$18,288
2024	$253,947	13.4	$18,951
2025	$249,096	12.7	$19,614
2026	$243,251	12.0	$20,271
2027	$236,359	11.4	$20,733
2028	$228,564	18.6	$12.288
2029	$229,253	17.6	$13,026
2030	$229,201	16.6	$13,807
2031	$228,318	15.6	$14,636
2032	$226,503	14.6	$15,514
2033	$223,648	13.6	$16,445
2034	$219,635	12.6	$17,431
2035	$214,336	11.6	$18,477
2036	$207,611	10.6	$19,586
2037	$199,307	9.6	$20,761
2038	$189,259	8.6	$22,007
2039	$177,287	7.6	$ 23,327
2040	$163,198	6.6	$24,727
2041	$146,779	5.6	$26,211
2042	$127,802	4.6	$27,783
2043	$106,020	3.6	$29,450

2044	$81,164	2.6	$31,217
2045	$52,944	1.6	$33,090
2046	$21,045	0.6	$21,045
Totals			$716,395

As you can see, in 2008 the IRA balance is $250,000. I've also included the life expectancy to show exactly how the numbers are calculated. Ed would be required to take an RMD of $10,121 in 2008. His distributions continue until 2021, where you will see a change in the life expectancy. This change is the result of Ed's death. The new factor is based on Bonnie's age. When Bonnie "inherits" the IRA, she has a lower RMD because she is two years younger than Ed. In 2027, Bonnie dies and the life expectancy changes again. The new life expectancy is based on David's age. A significant change occurs when David "inherits" the IRA from his mom. His payout becomes based on the IRS Single Lifetime Table for Inherited IRAs.

So, over Ed's, Bonnie's and David's lifetime, assuming a 6% constant rate of return, $716,395 will be distributed from Ed's IRA. It's important to realize that each distribution from the IRA is taxable. To better calculate the economic benefit received by Ed, then Bonnie and, finally, David, we need to adjust the payout from the IRA by the amount of tax likely paid from those distributions. If we assume a 25% federal tax and a 5% state tax, the total tax liability from all the distributions would be $214,918.50. Again, this includes both federal and state taxes. Based on that, Ed's IRA produced total after-tax income for himself and his family of $501,476.50. Not bad. But sit tight, we can do much better.

At the start of this chapter, we mentioned Ed and Bonnie's house. With a value of $225,000, you will see below that a reverse mortgage on the property using the HECM program would produce a lump sum of $137,707 tax free.

Your information
Borrower(s) Date of Birth: 2/1/1935; 3/1/1937
Home Value and Location: $225,000; 26062 HANCOCK
Total Property Loans and Liens: $0

Results

	HECM Monthly	HECM Annual
Lump Sum Advance		
Total Funds Available	$153,450	$126,225
Net Funds Available	$137,707	$111,064
Or a Credit Line Account		
Credit Line Available	$137,707	$111.064
Annual Growth Rate	3.5%	4.85%
Potential credit line in five years	$164,002	$141,475
Potential credit line in ten years	$195,316	$180,212
Or a monthly advance for as long as you live in your home		
Monthly Funds Available	$866	$796
Or any combination of lump sum at closing, credit line account, and monthly advance		

Let's discuss exactly how Ed can turn his $250,000 IRA into $1,400,000 *tax free*. The first step would be to qualify for a HECM reverse mortgage. Upon underwriting approval, Ed knows he has access to $137,707 to pay the tax on the conversion from a traditional IRA to a Roth IRA. Let's assume the federal tax cost of the conversion is 35%. On a $250,000 IRA, a 35% tax would be $87,500 federal tax due. For state tax purposes, we can use the 5% tax rate for $12,500 tax due. This brings our total tax outlay to an even $100,000.

In the face of a $100,000 tax bill, is this a wise financial move for Ed? If Ed doesn't want to take taxable required distributions from his IRA, the answer is yes. Furthermore, if Ed wants his IRA to benefit his wife and son and doesn't intend to spend the IRA money over his lifetime, the answer is absolutely yes.

The first benefit to explore with the Roth IRA is that there is no RMD. Since the tax is already paid, the Internal Revenue Service (IRS) has no incentive to require distribution. If it did, the distributions would be tax free, so why bother? Since there is no RMD for Ed or for Bonnie, they have the flexibility to take tax-free distributions when they need or want money with no mandatory schedule. And if they like, they can allow the Roth IRA to grow *tax free* for both their lifetimes without ever taking any money from the account. Look below at the Roth IRA Begin Value column. Ed will die in 2021 and the value, at a 6% compounded rate of return, will be $533,231. In 2027, Bonnie's assumed year of death, the balance is $756,399. This is *all tax-free* growth. The account value would be up, again assuming 6% steady growth, over $500,000 tax free.

Roth IRA Distributions: Alternative 1

Year	Benef. Age	Roth IRA Begin Value	Roth IRA Benef. Life Expectancy	Roth IRA Distributions	Cumulative Roth IRA Distributions
2008	71	$250,000	16.3	$0	$0
2009	72	$265,000	15.5	$0	$0
2010	73	$280,900	14.8	$0	$0
2011	74	$297,754	14.1	$0	$0
2012	75	$315,619	13.4	$0	$0
2013	76	$334,556	12.7	$0	$0
2014	77	$354,629	12.1	$0	$0
2015	78	$375,907	11.4	$0	$0
2016	79	$398,461	10.8	$0	$0

2017	80	$422,369	10.2	$0	$0
2018	81	$447,711	9.7	$0	$0
2019	82	$474,574	9.1	$0	$0
2020	83	$503,048	8.6	$0	$0
2021	84	$533,231	8.1	$0	$0
2022	62	$565,225	23.5	$0	$0
2023	63	$599,139	22.7	$0	$0
2024	64	$635,087	21.8	$0	$0
2025	65	$673,192	21.0	$0	$0
2026	66	$713,584	20.2	$0	$0
2027	67	$756,399	19.4	$0	$0
2028	68	$801,783	18.6	$43,107	$43,107
2029	69	$804,197	17.6	$45,693	$88,800
2030	70	$804,014	16.6	$48,435	$137,235
2031	71	$800,914	15.6	$51,341	$188,576
2032	72	$794,547	14.6	$54,421	$242,997
2033	73	$784,534	13.6	$57,686	$300,683
2034	74	$770,459	12.6	$61,148	$361,831
2052	92	$0	0.0	$0	$1,406,062
2053	93	$0	0.0	$0	$1,406,062
2054	94	$0	0.0	$0	$1,406,062
2055	95	$0	0.0	$0	$1,406,062
		$0	0.0	$0	$1,406,062

After Bonnie's death in 2027, David will be *required* to take distribution. Although Roth IRAs have no RMD, they do have Required Beneficiary Distributions (RBD) and they are based on the single life expectancy tables.

IRS unisex single like expectancies – ages 56-111+

Age of IRA owner Or Designated Beneficiary	Expectancy (Years)	Age of IRA owner Or Designated Beneficiary	Expectancy (Years)
56	28.7	84	8.1
57	27.9	85	7.6
58	27.0	86	7.1
59	26.1	87	6.7
60	25.2	88	6.3
61	24.4	89	5.9
62	23.5	90	5.5
63	22.7	91	5.2
64	21.8	92	4.9
65	21.0	93	4.6
66	20.2	94	4.3
67	19.4	95	4.1
68	18.6	96	3.8
69	17.8	97	3.6
70	17.0	98	3.4
71	16.3	99	3.1
72	15.5	100	2.9
73	14.8	101	2.7
74	14.1	102	2.5
75	13.4	103	2.3
76	12.7	104	2.1
77	12.1	105	1.9
78	11.4	106	1.7
79	10.8	107	1.5
80	10.2	108	1.4
81	9.7	109	1.2

| 82 | 9.1 | 110 | 1.1 |
| 83 | 8.6 | 111+ | 1.0 |

If we look at the year 2028, David will be 68 years old and have an IRS life expectancy of 18.6 years. In 2028, David will be required to take a *tax free* distribution of $43,107. The next year $45,693 - again, *tax free*. Over the 19- year period after his mother's death, David would receive $1,406,062 *tax free*.

This tremendous wealth creator requires no life insurance, but does something that, typically, can only be done with life insurance - *create tax free wealth for our children*!

If you have an IRA and want to see exactly how this strategy can help you - log onto our special readers only site - *www.goodbyeRMD.com*. There, you'll need to input, where applicable, your age, your spouse's age, the ages of your children, the value of your home, mortgage debt, zip code, first name, e-mail address and the rate of return you assume you'll earn over time. This entire process takes about two minutes. Within three days, you'll receive a *free* report specific to your IRA and a detailed analysis if this Free Money strategy can work for you.

Chapter 5 Fixing Fred & Wilma's Pension Pickle

Planning for retirement can be tricky. One of the most difficult decisions involves selecting your pension payout. Now, I am not talking about 401(k) plans or any other cash balance defined contribution plan. I am talking about a defined benefit pension, the monthly benefit your company pays out to you based on your years of service and salary, usually your last few years' of earned income before retirement. Your retirement age matters as well. So, there are many factors that determine your monthly pension benefit. Your company's human resource department can provide you with a variety of payout options. Among these are:

    1.) **A Straight Life Pension** – a pension that is payable for the life of the retired worker. The payout stops upon the retiree's death.

    2.) **A Joint and Survivor Pension** - a plan in which the retired worker receives a pension less than the amount in a straight life pension amount and in return, the surviving spouse will receive income after the retiree's death. Joint and survivor pensions are usually accompanied by a percentage such as 100%, 75%, 50% or 25%. To illustrate, if Roger (from the previous example) took a 50% survivor pension payout, he would have received $980 per month instead of the full $1,100 monthly benefit he would have received if he had elected the straight pension. This option would entitle Beth to receive $490 per month after Roger's death – 50% of Roger's $980.

The straight pension delivers the best deal when considering monthly retirement income only. When you consider the 30-plus years that people work to earn their pension, it's hard to forego hundreds of dollars each and every month to create a spousal guarantee. Plus, there is the risk that your spouse will die *before* you. If this happens, you usually cannot revert to a straight life pension. There are times, although rare, when a company will offer a "pop-up" election to cover this type of scenario. But even if your company offers a unique pop-up option, it still costs you something - there is no free lunch when it comes to pension planning from a company defined benefit plan. Additional protection always costs you some reduction in your monthly benefit payout. Anything besides a straight life pension will result in overall less monthly income from your pension.

Let's take a look at Fred and Wilma's retirement plan. Fred worked 40 years at the local mill in Pennsylvania, while Wilma spent her days raising her family of three boys. Both Fred and Wilma are 70 years old and in great shape. All three of their sons went on to college and now have good-paying careers. Fred and Wilma are very proud of their sons and love their seven grandchildren.

Financially, Fred did well considering all the expenses he incurred during the boys' college years. Each of his three boys graduated with a college education and no debt to repay. Mom and dad paid for their education and living expenses. Fred bought the family a nice home in an upscale neighborhood and everyone worked to keep the home in tip-top shape. Their home is now worth $278,000. Not bad, since Fred and Wilma bought the house years ago for only $36,000. Fred remembers his dad telling him how crazy he was for paying over $20,000 for a house. Boy, how times have changed.

Between investing in their children's education and keeping up their home, it was difficult to save money, but they did. Fred contributed to an IRA, which is currently worth $106,000, and Wilma's IRA, now worth about $58,000. Beyond the IRA accounts, they had little liquid cash - a little over $7,000 in their joint checking account. In addition to their assets, both Fred and Wilma enjoy Fred's excellent retirement income from his company pension:

Fred's Income:	
Social Security Fred	$1,340
Pension	$2,160
Fred's Total Income:	$3,500 per month

However, Fred's pension was established as a straight life pension and provided no residual benefit for Wilma after Fred's death. Wilma, on the other hand, received only social security. Her monthly income was $640. Combined, Fred and Wilma received $4,140 per month, with which they are enjoying a wonderful retirement. But, neither Fred nor Wilma ever stopped to consider how Wilma's financial situation would change should Fred die first.

This takes us back to Chapter 2 and the Social Security Shuffle, when a surviving spouse receives only the larger of the two social security checks when his/her spouse dies. In Wilma's case that would mean "inheriting" Fred's social security of $1,340, but losing her $640. Because Fred has a straight life pension, his $2,160 monthly pension check expires upon his death. From an income perspective, Wilma would go from household income of $4,140 to just Fred's social security amount of $1,340 - a reduction in household income of 68%. That's scary because life as Wilma knew it would be over. Her bills would be overwhelming and her only option would be to sell the home that she loves.

If Wilma dies before Fred, the scenario is quite different. Fred would keep his social security and his pension for a total of $3,500 a month. The only loss of income would be Wilma's $640 of social security income. Fred's loss of household income would be only 15%. A big difference. He could maintain his lifestyle and the 15% reduction would probably be absorbed by expenses directly attributable to Wilma's prior needs, expenses that after her death would be gone.

Faced with this reality, Fred didn't want to leave his wife in this type of financial situation. "How can we fix this?" Fred asked. "Actually, a better question, Matt, is can we afford to fix this?" I think we all worry about our ability to pay for things, even things we know we need. Free Money offers such an attractive solution because Free Money *never* becomes your children's liability. It's an asset based (your home) loan. Plus, when a couple applies for a reverse mortgage, the earliest loan repayment occurs after the *second death*. And if the economics don't favor the family, the loan doesn't get paid at all. The kids walk away and the house is forfeited. So, Fred and Wilma have a fantastic opportunity to solve this huge financial problem with a Free Money transaction.

Remember, the Free Money concept utilizes life insurance as a wealth creator. Fred's health makes applying for life insurance fairly easy. Before we assess how much coverage Fred can obtain, we first have to see how much money a reverse mortgage can generate to fund Fred & Wilma's transaction.

As mentioned, Fred and Wilma have a lovely home worth $278,000. Using the Wells Fargo calculator, we see that a HECM monthly reverse mortgage unlocks $153,658 of their home equity. Therefore, the amount of Free Money available from the reverse mortgage is $153,658. Since Fred is so healthy, a preferred rate is possible. A premium payment of $153,658, one time, could buy as much as $814,387. Imagine using the $153,658 of Free Money and turning it into $814,387 *tax free dollars*.

Your information
Borrower(s) Date of Birth: 2/10/1938; 5/11/1938
Home Value and Location: $278,000; 15222 ALLEGHENY
Total Property Loans and Liens: $0

Results

	HECM Monthly	HECM Annual	Home Keeper
Lump Sum Advance			
Total Funds Available	$170,496	$141,873	$62,767
Net Funds Available	$153,685	$125,681	$51,610
Or a Credit Line Account			
Credit Line Available	$153,685	$125,681	$51,160
Annual Growth Rate	4.37%	5.72%	0%
Potential credit line in five years	$191,140	$167,180	$51,160
Potential credit line in ten years	$237,724	$222,381	$51,160
Or a monthly advance for as long as you live in your home			
Monthly Funds Available	$939	$876	$422
Or any combination of lump sum at closing, credit line account, and monthly advance			

For Wilma, $814,387 is more than a lifetime of financial security. The question becomes, does it make sense to make that amount of money available to her? Now, before you ladies start calling me nasty names, what I am saying is that many years from now, after Fred passes, Wilma's health may change. It's possible that she may need long-term care. Long-term care costs today are typically $6,000 per month or more. But, who knows what they will be 15 or 20 years from now. So, $814,387 may sound like a lot of money today, but it might not last as long as you think if skilled nursing home care costs soar to $150,000 or more per year and Wilma needs that level of care. To squelch this bitter possibility, an interesting idea would be to again explore trust planning.

Fred could establish a specialized asset protection trust where upon his death Wilma would be entitled to all of the income from the death benefit – interest and dividends – but would not have direct access to the principal. The logic is, simply, if Wilma ends up in a skilled long-term care situation, the principal would not be available to pay for her care, thereby, making Wilma eligible for Medicaid because she has no access to these funds in a spend-down situation. The laws vary from state to state, so consult legal counsel in your state to verify. A provision that can be built into an asset protection trust is a set minimum rate of distribution, so if interest rates are really low, Wilma could set her minimum rate of distribution to be at least 5% of the original principal or the income generated, whichever is greater. Lawyers sometimes refer to this as a uni-trust provision and it protects the income beneficiary from lousy interest rates. Assuming Wilma's trust was designed this way, she would get income based on a 5% yield from the $814,387 asset or $40,719 per year – translating into $3,393.28 of monthly income for the rest of her life.

Let's go back to the household income figures we reviewed before:

Fred's Income:	
Social Security Fred	$1,340
Pension	$2,160
Fred's Total Income:	$3,500 per month

Fred's pension was elected at retirement as a straight life pension and it provides no residual benefit for Wilma after Fred's death. Wilma, on the other hand, receives only social security. So, her monthly income was $640. Together, their monthly household income is $4,140. However, with the Free Money transaction providing a $814,387 death benefit, Wilma, as a widow, would be financially protected with the following monthly income scenario:

Inherited Social Security from Fred	$1,340
Income from Trust at 5%	$3,393.28
Wilma's Income as a Widow:	$4,733.28 per month

This scenario is obviously much better than living just on Fred's social security of $1,340. In addition, their Free Money planning adds an $814,387 asset that their three sons can inherit when mom eventually passes away. As mentioned above, the trust can be structured in such a way that the income is payable to Wilma, but the life insurance death benefit principal is protected from a long-term care situation for their sons after mom dies. The boys then will have the option of paying the mortgage off – they'll have $814,387 tax free dollars to do so, if they choose. However, it's important to remind you they don't have to pay off the mortgage. If the balance is much higher than the market value, the boys can simply "walk away" with the $814,387 of tax free insurance proceeds.

If the value of the house is higher than the mortgage, they can initiate the sale of the house and keep any proceeds over and above the mortgage payoff. For Fred and Wilma, its great asset protection planning, it's great income protection planning for Wilma and it represents an amazing enhancement to their estate planning which dramatically benefits their children. Everyone wins with this plan. Fred and Wilma do not use any of their retirement income or any of their retirement assets to create the wealth inside of the trust – they only use the dead equity in their home – all while enjoying the benefits of home ownership.

Utilizing the right Free money transaction for your unique situation can make a huge difference, especially when one spouse has significant financial risk because of the loss of the main income earner's pension upon his or her death. This type of Free Money transaction can literally solve a very serious financial problem for the prudent retired couple. Now, Fred and Wilma get to enjoy 100% of Fred's retirement income and Wilma gets to keep that income after Fred is gone – truly an opportunity to "*Spend It Twice.*"

Chapter 6 Creating Income Out of Thin Air - Marla's Story

Marla is a healthy, active 78-year-old woman. She has been widowed for over 15 years, but keeps extremely busy with her kids and nine grandchildren. She enjoys her weekly golf match with the girls, followed by their traditional "after golf martini." Marla lives, from an outside observer's view, a very attractive retired life. The problem is that over the years her funds have been heavily depleted and her "inherited" income was limited to her husband Harry's social security. His lucrative company pension, a straight life pension, terminated when Harry died. Wanting to continue her life after Harry's death as it was when Harry was alive, Marla used the majority of her net worth to support her retirement activities.

At 78 years old Marla, is thrilled to have her health, vitality and mobility to enjoy life. However, at the same time, she is terrified about her future financial picture. She never believed that she would live this long and feel so healthy. Her greatest concern now is that her active lifestyle will need to be cut back to conform to her financial reality.

Marla has a beautiful home in a suburb of Pittsburgh, which has the same allure it did back when she and Harry bought the house after his "big promotion." She raised three wonderful children there, all of whom have excelled professionally and personally. One became a doctor; the other, a college professor and the youngest, an accountant. Each of Marla's children has three children of their own. Marla still spoils her children and grandchildren by doing special things for them, like taking them out to Sunday brunch. But, Marla has realized that the cost of the extras is exceeding her disposable income and wants to find a solution that allows her to continue her life on her own terms.

Marla's house has recently been appraised for $338,000. Based on her age and the location of the house, a reverse mortgage could offer her the following in the way of a HECM monthly lump sum settlement:

Your information
Borrower(s) Date of Birth: 3/21/1930
Home Value and Location: $338,000; 15143 ALLEGHENY
Total Property Loans and Liens: $0

Results

	HECM Monthly	HECM Annual
Lump Sum Advance		
Total Funds Available	$190,906	$166,763
Net Funds Available	$174,721	$151,019
Or a Credit Line Account		
Credit Line Available	$174,721	$151,019
Annual Growth Rate	4.42%	5.77%
Potential credit line in five years	$217,845	$201,385
Potential credit line in ten years	$271,613	$268,547
Or a monthly advance for as long as you live in your home		
Monthly Funds Available	$1,219	$1,174
Or any combination of lump sum at closing, credit line account, and monthly advance		

A note about the lender: Please be advised that I am using the Wells Fargo Reverse Mortgage Calculator because I am familiar with it. This is not an endorsement of Wells Fargo. AARP also has an excellent calculator. As mentioned, the FHA HECM program sets tight parameters that must be followed by all reverse mortgage lenders. The lender that you ultimately choose will offer you a similar, if not exact, loan structure. Most transactions occur through a mortgage broker.

From the chart, the HECM monthly loan will offer Marla $174,721 in a tax free lump sum. All *reverse mortgage proceeds are tax free*, because they are categorized as loan proceeds by the IRS for tax purposes. Marla has little else in the way of assets left, so this Free Money transaction needs to be expertly crafted to meet her long term needs and address her unique financial concerns, especially since she is in exceptional health and her life expectancy is greater than she anticipated years ago. Marla won't just be living long, she'll be living an active, healthy lifestyle. But, longevity is actually is one of Marla's greatest financial risk factors.

In discussing Free Money planning methods, Marla said that she has always wanted to leave the house intact for her children to inherit. She acknowledged that her other assets have been spent to support her lifestyle, but that she had always rationalized the house was the one asset she would preserve for her kids. She recalled the joyous feeling she had when she recently learned from an appraiser that the value of her home was over $300,000. "A very welcomed and wonderful surprise," she shared with me.

Often, an obstacle to a Free Money transaction is the perception that the house is lost in some way. That thinking is wrong. Free Money properly uses the house and then, at death, allows the family to take the house back and enjoy any additional appreciation gained during the reverse mortgage period. Free Money utilizes a person's insurability to create estate value that upon death is significantly greater than the future repayment of the mortgage. The difference between the ending mortgage balance and the life insurance death benefit defines how much Free Money a plan like Marla's creates for its user and, best of all, the proceeds are completely *tax free*. That it is tax free cannot be emphasized enough. In Marla's case, she wants to get a minimum of $338,000 of value for her children. We would recommend that Marla use the appropriate trust to protect this valuable asset from the possibility of a future disability or the need for expensive long-term care.

The first step to Marla's Free Money transaction is to apply for life insurance coverage in the amount of $338,000. The premium to purchase a $338,000 policy for a 78-year-old female in standard health is $136,356. We always shop the cost of life insurance coverage at a number of highly-rated carriers to insure the best price for the client. We look for the most competitive universal life products that you can use to guarantee coverage to specific ages. In Marla's case, we felt a contractual coverage guarantee through age 95 made the best sense because of her longer life expectancy. The one-time, single payment premium for the $338,000 of life insurance coverage used up $136,356 of the $174,721 of the reverse mortgage loan proceeds. This left us with $38,365 to create income for Marla.

Faced with having a little less than 22% of the loan proceeds to create income, our Free Money transaction needed to buy the annuity that would create the most income possible for the least amount of premium. In addition, Marla wanted to make sure she would receive income for the rest of her life. The right fit, based on Marla's goals, was the life only immediate annuity. Remember, the payments from this type of annuity stop upon the death of the annuitant. Therefore, Marla's income would stop when she died and there will be no residual benefit for her beneficiaries. From a beneficiary perspective, Marla is satisfying her desire to leave the value of the house to her kids.

None of Marla's children have a financial need for the family home, nor do they want to live there. For Marla, it's the principal of leaving the "value" of the home she built with her husband to their children, not the actual house. We emphasize again that any appreciation her home gains over and above the loan amount is payable to her heirs - her children. They are protected and will receive any upside appreciation of the real estate value of their family home plus the $338,000. Maximizing the beneficiary aspects of the income producing annuity is not necessary in this case because of the life insurance – otherwise, a life only annuity might not be the appropriate fit.

When buying an annuity, it always pays to shop, especially when purchasing a life only annuity. You should always check the credit quality of the insurer to identify the top carriers. You can do this easily through A.M. Best - *www.ambest.com* - or Standard & Poors - *www.standardandpoors.com*. Next, you need to request a quote for the amount the insurance company will be paying back to you each month for the rest of your life. Marla's comparison follows:

Death Benefit Before Payments Begin: None

Rank	Financial Institution	Monthly Income	Taxable Portion
1	Genworth Life Ins. Co.	$314.73	$72.39
2	American National Ins. Co.	$311.80	$69.53
3	Principal Financial Group	$311.26	$69.10
4	Protective Life Ins. Co.	$305.74	$63.59
	West Coast Life Ins. Co.	$305.74	$63.59
5	Integrity Life Ins. Co.	$299.53	$57.21
6	John Hancock Life	$299.45	$57.19
	Financial Institution		**Notes**
	Genworth Life Ins. Co.		A Proof of Birth list is generated for all illustrations containing life contingent benefits.
	John Hancock Life		Premium must be received within 60 days of application signed date.

As you can see, monthly benefit amounts vary from the different annuity companies. Based on the data provided above, it made sense to buy Marla's annuity from Genworth Life (formerly GE Financial) because the monthly income payment to Marla is the highest. An important aspect of an immediate annuity is how this type of annuity is taxed. For Marla, only $72.39 of each monthly payment is taxable. The remaining $242.34 of her $314.73 monthly income is tax free income that qualifies as the return of her own money. This tax preferential return of principal is helpful in protecting a retired person's social security from becoming taxable as the non-taxable portion of each monthly annuity payment is not counted in the social security taxation equation. As many are aware, social security was intended to be a tax-free benefit, but based on other sources of retirement income it can become up to 85% taxable. For Marla, only $72.39 per month is considered taxable income for a year-end total of $868.68 of interest income, even though she received $3,776.70 of total income from her annuity.

For Marla, using Free Money to create income made perfect sense. It provided her the peace of mind that the value of her home was going to be transferred to her children when she dies, while also leaving the upside appreciation of her lovely home to her family. Plus, Marla's transaction added $314.73 per month to her monthly retirement income. Did it make her rich? No, but it was just enough to afford her the financial wiggle room she needed to continue her weekly golf match and provide enough extras for her and her family to enjoy Sunday brunch once every few months – her treat.

It's important to understand that Marla wanted to buy insurance equal to the full value of her home. It's equally important to realize her mortgage balance may not grow to the full home value. If the final mortgage balance is less than her home value, Marla's planning will have actually created additional wealth for her children above and beyond leaving them just the value of the family home. Had she crafted her plan a little more in favor of her income, she could have easily increased her monthly income $500 or more each month. In some circumstances, a Free Money transaction may purchase only an income paying immediate annuity. The reverse mortgage also offers its own annuity payout, so it's important to compare the income option of the mortgage versus what is commercially available on the immediate annuity market. Most importantly, Free Money can literally create income from the dead equity trapped in a retiree's home without losing any of the benefits of home ownership. Certain situations may require no life insurance. A plan without life insurance would create considerably more monthly income.

Chapter 7 The Ultimate Estate & Elder Planning Technique

"Matt, thank you for helping my mom. Now show me how to make sure this never happens to me and my family." I can't tell you the number of adult children who have thanked me for helping to provide for their elderly parents after a financial crisis caused by a long-term care need or the family's realization that because of progressing dementia, their loved one would require care sooner than expected. In nearly every situation, we've always been able to develop a plan to protect their mom or dad's health care benefits and, additionally, make sure that their mom or dad (sometimes both) never would run out of money and out of options. Because, remember, "When you are out of money you are out of options." The techniques used at my financial firm are used by some of America's best elder law attorneys and are *not* the target of this chapter. The target here is to address the almost inevitable final words from the adult children after we help their parents. "I want to schedule an appointment with you so you can show us how to make sure this never happens to us and our children." I consider this extremely valuable material for those readers who are more newly retired and those soon to be retired.

For an example of the ultimate estate and elder plan, we'll assume that both partners in our example couple are 65 years old. At that age, we can do a reverse mortgage, Free Money applies. We may yield a slightly smaller result from the reverse mortgage, but their youth will make the insurance considerably less expensive, so fewer dollars will still buy our couple a lot more life insurance coverage. We can also apply new "add-ons" that the insurance industry has created to address the issue of long term care. I'll explain these "add-ons" in detail as you read on.

We'll name our next couple Jack and Jill. Let's lay out their assets and income so we can plan off of these variables:

Assets:	
Joint Brokerage Account	$300,000
Jack's IRA	$90,000
Jill's IRA	$85,000
Joint Checking & Savings	$25,000
Total Liquid Assets:	$500,000
House Value	$278,000

Income:	
Jack's Social Security	$1,540 per month
Jack's Pension	$2,200 per month*
Jill's Social Security	$780
Total Household Income:	$4,520
Income To Jill If Jack Dies:	$1,540 (66% reduction)
Income to Jack If Jill Dies:	$3,740 (17% reduction)

* Jack's pension is a straight single life pension with no spousal beneficiary benefits after his death.

We'll assume neither Jack nor Jill owned any life insurance prior to this planning. They have two adult children, who live a considerable distance away. Both children are successful professionals with solid marriages and healthy children. Jack's primary planning goal is to have an enjoyable retirement and to make sure Jill is cared for if he dies before her. Jill wants to create an estate to benefit her children and grandchildren. From a goal setting perspective, Jack and Jill were *not* on the same page. Jack's primary focus was on Jill and himself, whereas, Jill would do without to benefit her family.

The question that always comes up is, "Should we own long-term care insurance?" The answer is that long-term care insurance can be a very valuable type of coverage to own *if* you need long-term care payment assistance in the future. But, it begs to have the question asked and answered, *"What if you don't need long-term care in the future?"* Long-term care insurance pays out a monthly benefit when you make a claim for care costs. Some policies include benefit payments for home health, assisted living, and long-term acute care such as skilled nursing home care. I believe it's natural for us to want a long-term care plan that keeps us in the comfort of our own home as long as possible. *With this in mind, it's important to carefully review the benefit payout clauses in our long-term care policies because it is critical to understand what the policy pays for, when the policy starts to pay out and how much we can expect from the policy based on our care needs.* The majority of new clients I meet with have never read their long-term care insurance policies. Their understanding of the coverage is based on what the agent told them. Always be sure that what is said is exactly the same as what is in writing. Taking an agent's 'word for it' can have extreme consequences. I am not suggesting the agent is being deceptive. To the contrary, I believe most agents want to do well by their clients, but may not have fully understood the internal make-up of the *legal contract.*

Traditional long-term care insurance, frankly, doesn't thrill me because it fails to answer the second question, "What if I don't need care?" All of the premiums paid into the long-term care insurance result in *no* benefit if long-term care is not needed.

So, not needing care after buying long-term care insurance represents 100% cost and 0% benefit. In addition, long-term care insurance is experience rated, much the way insurance companies price automobile and homeowners insurance. If big storms damage homes in your area, the experience of the insurance company is not profitable. At that point, the company makes a request to the insurance commissioner of your state and probably gets a rate increase. Long-term care insurance works the same way. If an insurance company insures a large number of 75-year-olds and more 75-year-olds than expected need care sooner than the company actuaries originally believed, then the premium on your long-term care insurance can be increased. So, long-term care insurance fails from my perspective on the budgeting front, because as we age we typically live on a fixed income and an increase in long-term care insurance cost is financially prohibitive. Also, increases in premiums often lead to a discontinuation of the coverage at ages when the insured is more likely to need the benefits.

Flaws in long-term care coverage, in my opinion, can be fixed by a new generation of life insurance policies currently being issued. These polices offer an "add on" benefit, also known as a rider, that allows the insured to pay a portion of the death benefit each month into a long-term care insurance benefit and deduct that long-term care benefit from the death benefit. This makes the coverage much more affordable and prevents the benefit from being lost if the insured does not need long-term care. This new generation "add-ons" allows you to use the policy for long-term care, if needed. If not, it is paid to your heirs as a life insurance death benefit.

The rider is an extremely attractive option for retirees and healthy, middle age professionals because it offers an either/ or benefit. If you become disabled it will act as your long-term care policy and provide you a monthly benefit to help you pay your care costs. If you don't need long- term care, it pays out at your death as a life insurance death benefit payable to your beneficiaries, tax free. This represents a huge advantage over traditional long- term care insurance. Another significant benefit of this type of coverage over traditional long-term care insurance is how the premiums for the rider can be purchased. The cost is fixed at the time of purchase. This is something that cannot be done when buying long-term care insurance. It's important enough to repeat - the price of traditional long-term care insurance is based on the insurance companies' *experience* and, therefore, premiums can go up if the experience of the insurer warrants a price increase. Therefore, if your insurance company also insured a large number of policyholders who needed long-term care sooner than anticipated, then your cost will probably increase.

But with long-term care coverage utilizing the life insurance rider attached to a universal life policy, your cost is fixed. With this added rider, you have the luxury of life insurance and/or long-term care, depending on what you ultimately need. You won't have to choose between the two. This is a much better solution to insuring long-term care.

As for Jack and Jill, their plan includes long term care funded by the purchase of two no-lapse guarantee universal life contracts, one insuring Jack and the other insuring Jill. The contracts include the specifically-designed rider described above that pays *2% of the death benefit monthly* in the event they are unable to perform two or more of the activities considered normal for daily living: bathing, eating, continence, toileting, dressing and transferring. The contracts do not require care to be in a skilled nursing home to pay the benefit, just that two of the six primary activities of daily living cannot be met. The benefit starts to pay out at a rate of 2% of the death benefit per month as soon as a physician provides certification to the insurer that the insured will likely need extended care for the rest of the insured's life. The physician will be asked to renew the certification for care annually.

Let's look at the economics. At 65, Jack and Jill can qualify for a Free Money transaction using a reverse mortgage. By owning a $278,000 home in Pittsburgh, they are eligible for a $144,388 lump sum HECM monthly reverse mortgage. As a reminder, Jill and Jack will make *no* monthly payment on their reverse mortgage - the interest will accrue over time based on the US one-year T-bill rates.

Your information
Borrower(s) Date of Birth: 3/18/1943; 6/23/1943
Home Value and Location: $278,000; 15090 ALLEGHENY
Total Property Loans and Liens: $0

Results

	HECM Monthly	HECM Annual
Lump Sum Advance		
Total Funds Available	$161,536	$124,699
Net Funds Available	$144,388	$108,284
Or a Credit Line Account		
Credit Line Available	$144,388	$108,284
Annual Growth Rate	4.42%	5.77%
Potential credit line in five years	$180,025	$144,397
Potential credit line in ten years	$224,458	$192,553
Or a monthly advance for as long as you live in your home		
Monthly Funds Available	$823	$717
Or any combination of lump sum at closing, credit line account, and monthly advance		

Jill's one-time single payment premium for $200,000 worth of life insurance coverage, including the long-term care rider, is $58,418. Jack's premium was higher at $64,482 for the same $200,000 in coverage because men, typically, have a shorter life expectancy than women and, therefore, are required to pay higher premiums.

Please be aware that the pricing of a life insurance policy premium is based on many factors. Therefore, please view this example as a general review of the concept as terms and conditions of coverage will most likely be different in every case.

As a quick review, Jack and Jill have a total of $500,000 of liquid invested assets. Of this, $300,000 is in a joint account; $120,000 in Jack's IRA, and the remaining $80,000 in Jill's IRA. If you recall, Jack has much greater retirement income, whereas Jill faces very serious financial strain after Jack's death due to her dramatically reduced income as a widow. So, let's examine the impact of their Free Money transaction assuming long-term care is never needed for Jack or Jill.

In the event that Jack dies before Jill we calculated her income as a widow to be $1,540 per month, as you can see below:

Income:	
Jack's Social Security	$1,540 per month
Jack's Pension	$2,200 per month*
Jill's Social Security	$780
Total Household Income:	$4,520
Income To Jill If Jack Dies:	$1,540 (66% reduction)
Income to Jack If Jill Dies:	$3,740 (17% reduction)

* Jack's pension is a straight single life pension with no spousal beneficiary benefits after his death.

So, Jill would have to make her financial ends meet while having only 34% of their former household income. This obviously will not be possible and Jill's lifestyle will seriously diminish. However, with the addition of the $200,000 life insurance benefit on Jack, Jill now adds an additional $200,000 of tax free assets to her portfolio. If we assume Jack lives another 15 years until age 80 and then dies, Jill would then have a 9.11 year average life expectancy (for an 80-year-old female).

Jill's lost income of $2,980 per month (calculated by subtracting her current household income of $4,520 from her future survivor income of $1,540) can be significantly supplemented by Jack's $200,000 death benefit. Even without adding interest to the $200,000, the death benefit could be placed into an annuity that would cover the $2,980 per month shortfall for 67 months. To calculate, simply divide $200,000 by the monthly income shortfall of $2,980. This takes care of Jill's financial needs for 67 months of her 109 month life expectancy. So, there is no need yet to dip into her invested or saved assets. She is able to spend the $200,000 death benefit Free Money first. Now remember, Jill is still living in the house. The assets that Jill accumulated with Jack over their lifetime will still be intact and waiting for her use if she lives beyond 67 months. At some point, this planning will result in her children getting more money than they would have otherwise inherited because $200,000 tax free dollars came into Jill's financial picture upon Jack's death.

Now for Jack, his income loss is much less than Jill's if she were to die first, so he has plenty of family gifting options to benefit his children to consider. He has the flexibility to take more income or use that asset any way he believes is in his or his family's best interests. Free Money transactions always keep options open and allow incredible flexibility.

Let's see what would happen if Jack becomes disabled. Jill would have tremendous financial risk. With skilled nursing home costs at $6,000 or more a month in most parts of the country, it wouldn't take Jack and Jill long to lose a considerable amount of hard-earned assets. Jill is especially at risk because her husband's income is much greater than hers. In the event he has a very long need for skilled care and their assets were depleted, Jill's income would be set by a federal guideline known as the Minimum Monthly Maintenance Needs Allowance (MMMNA) which in 2008 was $1,712 per month.

Note: Some states, like Illinois, automatically award a maximum Community Spousal Resource Allowance (CSRA). This means that the first $109,560 going to the surviving spouse is automatically protected by regulation. The MMMNA could be as high as $2,610.

This shows that if Jack's disability ended up costing a significant portion of their liquid net worth, the financial pain is not limited to just assets. After being impoverished to pay for his care, Jill would get only a small percentage - $1,712 per month of the $4,520 or 37.9% - of their collective household income. This type of crisis can be avoided by using the Free Money concept.

Now, personal care costs are always rising, but if Jack becomes disabled and has a life insurance policy with an appropriate long term care rider and he was unable to perform at least two activities of daily living, then he could get $4,000 per month to help pay for his care. It is really important for you to understand he does *not* need to be in a skilled nursing home facility. What I love most about this plan is that failing at two of the six activities of daily living is the critical hurdle to unlocking the long-term care financial benefits. A physician attests, in writing, that at least two of the tests were failed and that the type of disability is considered permanent. Unlike traditional long-term care insurance, where bills have to be submitted and payments from the insurance carrier need to match the actual cost of care, this life insurance rider simply pays 2% of the death benefit monthly upon the company's review and acceptance of a physician's statement. Consider this possibility. Perhaps Jill needs a lot of help with Jack, but wants to keep him at home. This benefit provides Jill with $4,000 per month to help pay for in-home care. If Jack's disability progresses, the $4,000 each month could be used to help pay for a comfortable assisted living facility. The coverage at 2% long-term care benefit payout per month lasts for 50 months (2% x 50 payments = 100% of the death benefit). In Jacks case, $200,000 at $4,000 per month will last for 50 months.

So, Jack's benefit can come to him as either a long-term care benefit or a life insurance benefit - *or both*. What if Jack needs long-term care assistance for 25 months and then dies? Well, $100,000 would have been paid out as long-term care benefits. The remaining $100,000 of the $200,000 life insurance benefit is paid out as tax free death benefit to his named beneficiary, Jill.

The ultimate plan does require good health in order to qualify for the life insurance, which is medically underwritten. Your ability to qualify for this type of coverage is based on your medical records and, typically, some type of examination. The exam may include blood work, an EKG and other testing. The larger the amount of life insurance policy, the more in-depth the medical exam requirements will be. So, there is a benefit to starting young and I encourage you to let your youth work for you.

Below you'll see various annual payments for $300,000 of this type of coverage:

Age Purchased:	Male – Preferred NT		Female – Preferred NT	
	Death Benefit Without Life Access Accelerated Benefits Rider		Death Benefit Without Life Access Accelerated Benefits Rider	
Age 35	$1,627.60	$1,814.55	$1,344.60	$1,547.25
Age 45	$2,404.56	$2,664.33	$1,877.22	$2,167.99
Age 50	$2,854.48	$3,154.20	$2,363.43	$2,716.96
Age 55	$3,705.35	$4,087.59	$3,022.56	$3,468.56
Age 65	$6,229.75	$6,845.58	$5,070.87	$5,946.70

Unlike the Free Money concepts, younger buyers need to pay for the coverage out of their assets or income. Still, it pays to buy young. One way is to structure your payments as low as possible until age 62 and then pay the remaining premium on your life insurance policy in a lump sum using reverse mortgage proceeds the Free Money way. This way, you get the benefit of a lower price while young, even though the cost is still "out-of-pocket." The risk factor with this payment plan would be if the FHA pulled the reverse mortgage offering and it wasn't available to you when you turned age 62. In my opinion, it is very unlikely that the FHA would eliminate the HECM program and deny future retirees access to this unique financing to help supplement their retirement.

In the next chapter, my good friend Rick Law, an elder law attorney, analyzes the legal ramifications of this type of plan. Elder law is a specialized practice of law geared toward helping seniors with issues ranging from dealing with disabilities to qualifying for benefits from Medicare, Medicaid, the Veterans Administration and other sources. Rick is rightfully regarded as one of the very best in his field and is the founder of the Veterans Benefit Institute of Chicago and a partner in a website devoted to helping caregivers to family members with Alzheimers – *www.alzheimershope.com.*

Rick's career as an elder law attorney started with a phone call from his friend Louise May. "Rick, Bob has been diagnosed with Alzheimer's. What are we going to do? Am I going to lose my home? Are we going to lose everything?" she asked. Nine years later, Rick has become one of the most sought after "teachers" to other elder law attorneys and each day his firm, Law ElderLaw, is dedicated to providing the answers that "throw a lifeline" to individuals and families in danger of sinking under the weight of long-term care cost burdens.

Chapter 8 Never Out of Money, Never Out of Options

After reading the last seven chapters, it should be clear to you that Matt Zagula wants you to live long and to live well. He's a financial advisor and based on my experience working with Matt and at least 200 clients, I have found him to be extremely innovative, capable and honest. He has assisted me and my team at Law ElderLaw, LLP (*www.lawelderlaw.com*) as we work to provide the best legal and financial solutions for families who have been hit with the crushing burden of long-term illness.

I am an elder law attorney. Elder law is a relatively new area of legal practice in the American legal system. It began some time in the late 1980s. In fact, the National Academy of Elder Law Attorneys is celebrating its 20th anniversary this year. Elder law came into existence because of the reality that many people no longer die suddenly from issues like heart attack and stroke. Since the 1960s, the average life expectancy in the US has increased almost 20 years! Given that, tens of millions of individuals will live into their 80s, 90s and beyond.

It is inappropriate to look to yesterday's solutions to try to solve today's and tomorrow's problems. The seniors of today and the baby boomer seniors of tomorrow face a situation that is totally new and for which there are no good models. None of the current public or private support systems are adequate to take care of the millions of Americans who are now living long enough to become the "old old." Therefore, it's up to you to do the research - and then take the actions necessary - to give you and your loved ones a better chance of never being out of money and never being out of options before you're out of breath.

I work with financial advisors, medical professionals, long-term care managers and those brave and sacrificing family members who give so much to care for their loved ones who are dealing with Alzheimer's, Parkinson's, ALS, Huntington's disease, multiple sclerosis and a host of other illnesses which affect either an individual's mobility or memory or both.

People sometimes ask me how I had the foresight to enter a field of law which is dramatically expanding when the economy is contracting. The answer is that I did *not* go looking for elder law, it came looking for me. About nine years ago, friends and family started turning to me to help them understand how they were going to preserve their home, lifestyle and dignity when presented with the never-ending costs associated with long-term care and the never-ending need for services by those afflicted by long term care illnesses.

To do this, one has to understand the interchange between the following:

1) Health care / caregiver needs of the client
2) The federal rules of taxation regarding investments
3) The federal rules related to public benefits such as Medicare, Medicaid, and Social Security
4) Benefits for veterans over 65, blind, and/or disabled
5) Wills, revocable living trusts, various asset protection irrevocable trusts, powers of attorney and other advance directives
6) Family dynamics and mediation
7) Financial products appropriate for individuals afflicted with long-term illnesses.

When I review this list that I've created above, it makes me take a deep breath. The elder law attorney has to keep in mind an amazing panorama of concerns when working with individuals who are facing a long-term care crisis. It is important to understand that while the person with a long-term care need is normally the one who is our client, they are very concerned about the effect their illness is having on their loved ones. When I meet with clients, I look across the table into the eyes of individuals who are afraid that they are going to wind up out of money and out of quality health care options. They look to me and their financial advisors to try to help them find some way to make sure they can continue to lead a quality life. I truly wish I had a magic wand.

Matt has been working for many years to help the same types of families that come to my office every single day. He sees the same problems that the elder law attorney faces, but his work is focused on how to make the best financial decisions. Our profession should complement his work by providing the best *legal* solutions so that a client is able to obtain the public benefits which will allow them to have the best lifestyle possible. Collaboration between the elder law attorney and the financial advisor yields the best solutions.

Since you're reading this book, I have to assume that you are like most of my clients. You are analytical, concerned, and prone to take action. I congratulate you on reading this important material so that you can learn these new concepts, which have such great potential. It can help you to put to work what was referred to herein as the "dead equity" in your home. This is the economic spark plug necessary to carry out a variety of plans to help you address your financial worries. *Spend It Twice* has given you, the reader, examples of how to use a combination of financial products to provide a better lifestyle for the surviving spouse after the death of the first individual. Since I'm a male, I often look across the table at the husbands and wives and say to them, quite bluntly, "You know, we don't know how we're going to die, but I guarantee you that we're going to die one of two ways. We're either going to die quickly or we're going to get some sort of long-term disease and in that case, our care will be very expensive over a long period of time. And we men usually die first and leave you women with a mess to clean up."

Now, it's impossible for us to sit here today and predict with any certainty what type of death any one of us is going to have. But, we need to prepare for the reality that we may die quickly or we may have long-term care needs and expenses. Therefore, our estate plan and our financial plan need to be designed so they work well regardless of *which* type of death comes our way. In addition, we should create a plan that does not leave our beloved spouse in a mess or with a mess to clean up.

Traditional estate planning often is no more than "death planning." It seldom focuses on the real issues of what happens if I *don't* die, but instead face months or, possibly, years of expenses in the range of $5,000 to $10,000 a month for long-term care. Therefore, one purpose of Matt's advice is to help people understand what they can do to maximize their financial outcomes so that they are properly prepared for the long term.

You may not realize this, but Medicare was set up in 1964 to provide seniors funds to cover their health care needs. The government really believed that it was enacting a health care system that would prevent American seniors and their loved ones from being impoverished by health care expenses. What went wrong fulfilling that goal? The answer is that in 1964, most men and women died before the age of 70 from things such as heart attack, stroke, and cancer. So the Medicare system was designed primarily to pay only for *short-term illnesses*. Medicare pays only if there is a corresponding "Medicare reimbursement code" to reimburse the health care provider. Take note that there is *no* Medicare reimbursement code for long-term care either at home, in assisted living, or in nursing home facilities.

In the 1960s, there weren't as many people who "died of old age." But now, in 2009, medical science can lessen the chance of dying from heart attack, stroke, and cancer. People's lives can be *maintained*, albeit often at great expense, so that they will live into their 80s, 90s and beyond. But, Medicare is not there for your long-term care. I don't think most seniors understand that.

And because Medicare does not pay for your long-term health care, you are faced with the reality of paying for it yourself until you reach a point where you become impoverished. And that's where Medicaid takes over. Although Medicaid is the primary payer of nursing home expenses in the US, it was not originally designed to be so. It is really a program designed to pay for medical treatment when an individual has exhausted all other resources. If you wind up on Medicaid, you probably are out of money and, therefore, out of options. In order to qualify for Medicaid, you must, as a single person, have no more than $2,000 to your name and depending in which state you live, you will be restricted to a monthly personal needs allowance between $30 and $90. You may be saying to yourself, "How could they do that?" Basically what happens when you go on Medicaid is that you are placed in the same economic class as the homeless. They, too, are out of money and out of options.

Have you ever volunteered to serve at a homeless shelter? Volunteering there has shown me that I never want to be in their situation. I never want to be out of money. And we all know when you're out of money, you are out of quality options – options that give life its vitality, lift and delight. Interestingly, the homeless ones that I have met never chose to live a life on the streets. Rather, they're on the streets because of the consequences of bad decisions, bad luck or bad genetics. But for all of them, they are where they are because they are out of money and options. And when you have no capital to invest, it's hard to recover and get back into the mainstream. So, when I see the homeless and how their situation is similar to those of many seniors who face a life without adequate health care and without adequate finances, I am very aware that it's my job to do the best I can to help people make the right decisions so they are never out of money and never out of quality options.

Just yesterday, a woman who is at home taking care of her husband with Alzheimer's asked me, "Should I take my social security check when I'm 62 or should I wait until I'm 65 when it would be higher?" She is one of the courageous caregivers who have given up her job to stay at home to care for her husband who has early onset Alzheimer's disease. Neither she nor her husband is yet 62 years of age and given his condition, he will probably die before her. I said, "Do you realize that when your husband dies, you will not receive *two* social security checks any more, but rather you will receive only one?" She responded, "You're kidding, right?" No, I wasn't! When a spouse dies, you will receive the larger of the two checks - one check, not two.

Now you can see why many seniors wind up out of money and out of options. None of them directly chose a life of existing on social security, Medicare or Medicaid. When you live on these resources, you have very little money and very few quality options. Today, you can consider future realities and make choices to safeguard your spending power for today and tomorrow.

The "*Spend It Twice*" Free Money concept consists of two, possibly three, separate financial transactions:

1) A lump-sum reverse mortgage
2) The purchase of a single premium universal life insurance policy
3) The purchase of an annuity to provide monthly income for you or your spouse after your death

We have all heard the phrase, "There is no such thing as a free lunch," and it should be obvious that there is no such thing as "free money." There are transaction costs associated with each financial product used to fund the *Spend It Twice* investment. You should choose qualified financial advisors who will provide you with a full disclosure of all fees related to products and services. Even though there is no "free lunch," Matt Zagula's financial recipe is based on combining three distinct ingredients - reverse mortgage, single premium universal life insurance and annuities - that have financial benefits that can be calculated with a high degree of certainty. This outcome predictability means that you can avoid the risk element of the volatile stock and bond market by using the *Spend It Twice* strategy.

Today's seniors face a daunting future that requires them to make good choices to maximize the value of their assets and minimize risk. We must all be self-reliant in preparing for the future.

Please make the right choice today to ensure that neither you nor your loved ones are "on the streets." As an elder law attorney, I look in the eyes of the frail, the disabled and the courageous. My job is to help my clients achieve their goals of living a life with dignity. No one wants to be out of money before they are out of breath. I heartily recommend that you engage capable professionals to help you prepare for the inevitability of mortality and aging. Follow Matt's advice and maximize your financial estate. Then, couple that with an estate plan designed for both long-term illness asset protection and post-death legacy goals. It's a new day, and it's time to act to protect your home, your health care and the loved ones who will survive you.

Rick Law
Attorney at Law
Chicago, Illinois

WA